The Exciting Number 8

A Birthday Number Book

by Karin Snelson

Illustrated by Peter Georgeson

Andrews McMeel Publishing

Kansas City

An octopus has eight arms.

Imagine yourself swimming in the ocean. Suddenly, you brush up against something squishy! Something with eight arms! And suction cups! The arms are wrapping around you! Oh nooooo, it's an octopus!

The octopus has many wonderful tricks:
- An octopus can see in all directions without turning its head.
- When an octopus needs to hide, it can change to look like a rough, dark rock, or like smooth pale sand.

- When startled, an octopus can squirt out a cloud of dark ink to escape from its enemies.
- An octopus turns a deep pink color when it's excited.
- An octopus can scoot backward at high speed!

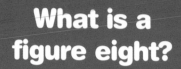

What do gray reef sharks and figure skaters have in common? They can both move in a figure-eight pattern! A figure eight looks just like the number eight.

The figure eight is an important move in figure skating. It is made up of two perfect circles. A figure skater begins and ends each circle at the same spot on the ice.

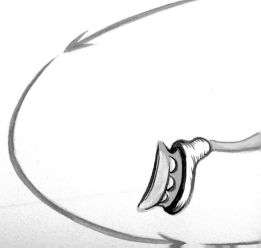

Start here

Put your finger on the starting part of the "8" you see here. Move your finger along the "8" shape. That pattern is called a *figure eight*.

The gray reef shark sometimes swims in a figure eight when it is frightened.

There are eight notes in a musical octave.

Have you ever heard the song, "Old MacDonald Had a Farm"? Here is how it looks in musical notation:

There are eight notes in a musical *octave*. Have you ever sung "Do-re-mi-fa-so-la-ti-do"? Do (DOE), re (RAY), mi (MEE), fa (FAH), so, la, ti (TEE) and do represent eight notes, or *tones*, that can make up an octave. On a piano, if you put your left thumb on middle C and stretched your little finger up eight notes to the next highest C note on the keyboard, that would be an octave! Of course, an octave can begin on any note.

Hawaii has eight major islands.

Hawaii is not at all like the other 49 states of the United States. For one thing, it's stuck all by itself in the Pacific Ocean. The capital of Hawaii, Honolulu, is 2,397 miles (3,857 kilometers) away from San Francisco, California.

The state of Hawaii is made up of 132 islands, but the eight major islands in Hawaii are: *Hawaii* (or the Big Island), *Maui* (MOW-ee), *Oahu* (oh-AH-hoo), *Kauai* (kuh-WHY-ee), *Molokai* (MOLE-uh-kai), *Lanai* (lah-NA-ee), *Niihau* (NEE-ee-how), and *Kahoolawe* (kah-HO-oh-LAH-vay).

The Hawaiian islands were all formed by volcanoes. In fact, two of the biggest volcanoes on Earth are on the island of Hawaii: *Mauna Loa* (MAH-na-LOW-uh) and *Kilauea* (KIL-oh-AY-uh).

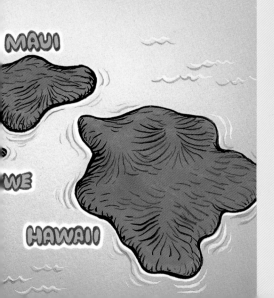

MAUI

WE

HAWAII

All spiders have eight legs.

Spiders are not insects, because insects—like flies, ants, and bees—have six legs. Instead, spiders are *arachnids*. Arachnids are a part of a group of animals called *arthropods*, that have jointed legs and hard outer cases called *exoskeletons*.

Many spiders have eight eyes, too, and they can see bugs that are behind them.

Most spiders eat insects, and many build silky webs to catch them. The spider sits perfectly still in the middle of its web until it feels some unlucky bug fly into its sticky trap. Then the spider runs over and wraps the bug up in silk, bites it with its fangs, and sucks out its insides. Delicious!

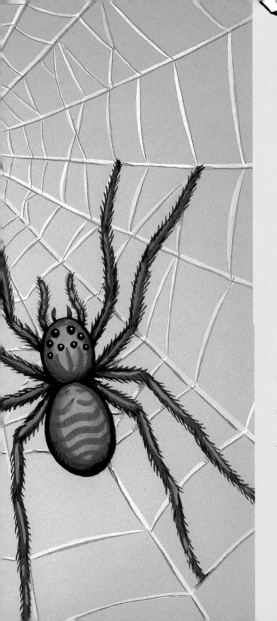

Little Miss Muffet was a real person. Her father was a spider expert named Thomas Muffet who used to make his daughter eat mashed spiders as medicine, whenever she had a cold.

NEPTUNE

Neptune is the fourth-largest planet in the solar system, but you can't see it from Earth. Even when viewed with a telescope the planet looks like a fuzzy blue dot. This is why no one knew that Neptune existed until

Neptune is not always the eighth planet from the Sun, because once in a while it changes places with the ninth planet, Pluto. This is because of the way the orbits of the two planets are shaped. For about 20 years out of every 248 years, Neptune is the *ninth* planet from the Sun!

the early 1800s. Neptune is a giant gas planet, and it has several faint rings and eight moons. One of Neptune's moons, Triton, has active volcanoes on it.

Pizza for eight!

Did you know that the first pizza was made in Italy in the 1800s? Since then, pizza has been one of the world's favorite foods!

How many pieces of pizza can you eat? Is your choice a large, a medium, or a small? Do you like it covered in pepperoni, or mozzarella cheese, or both? No matter how you slice it or how many slices you can eat, pizza is almost always cut into eight pieces.

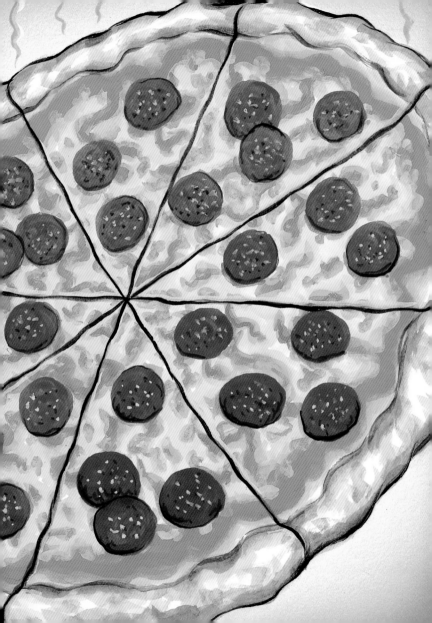

August is the eighth month.

August is the warmest month of the year. It's a great time for pool parties and barbecues in the backyard. But most of all, August is a great month for sleeping outside in a tent or curled up in a sleeping bag—looking at the stars and listening to the crickets as they sing you to sleep.

August is usually the last month of summer vacation. You could spend it having fun or getting ready for school. Which will you pick?

Eight glasses of water a day.

When you are eight, it's important to take care of yourself. One of the most important things you can do is to drink lots of water. Water is like a bath for your insides, and helps to keep all those flu bugs and colds washed away.

Eight glasses of water is a good way to make sure that you are getting all the water that your body needs every day. So keep a large bottle of water in the refrigerator and have a nice cold drink every time you think of it.

Have you ever been "behind the eight ball?"

In the game of pool, the eight ball is a solid black ball with a big eight in the middle of it. The eight ball is just one of 15 balls, but it's a really important one! For one thing, the eight ball can make you lose the whole game if you hit it in the pocket too early. That's why when you say "I'm behind the eight ball," it means that you are in a very uncomfortable position!

A pair of skates has eight wheels.

There are eight wheels on a pair of skates. Sometimes the wheels are side by side, but sometimes they are all in a line—and those kinds of skates are called *in-line skates*. That means that the wheels are set in a line along the bottom of the skates.

No matter what kind of skates you prefer, it is important to always wear a helmet to protect your head! You should also wear knee and elbow pads, too, for those times when those eight little wheels have a mind of their own.

An *octagon* is a shape with eight sides.

You probably see octagons every day, because stop signs have eight sides. You might even wear octagonal glasses!

Octo means "eight" in the Latin language. An octagon has eight sides, an *octopus* has eight legs, and an *octave* has eight notes. An *octet* is a singing group of eight people. An *octodont* is a kind of rodent with eight teeth. Can you find any other words in the dictionary that begin with *oct*?

Three little words, eight little letters.

What are the most treasured three words in the English language that are also made up of eight letters? They are words and letters that you see on a valentine in February, and something that your mom or dad says when you are being put to bed! More than that, they have a magical way of making you feel warm inside when you say them and hear them. What are they?
I LOVE YOU!

Love
you!

Now you are eight years old!

I f you traveled to different parts of the world today, people might say "Happy birthday!" to you, and ask you how old you are. Here's how people might say this in Spanish, French, and German, and how you would answer.

Happy birthday! How old are you?
I am eight years old.

¡Feliz cumpleaños! ¿Cuantos años tienes?
Tengo ocho años.

Bonne anniversaire! Quel âge as-tu?
J'ai huit ans.

Glücklicher Geburtstag! Wie alt bist du?
Ich bin acht Jahre alt.